Conisbrough Ca

Steven Brindle and Agnieszka Sadraei

CONTENTS

Tour of the Castle

SETTING

The story of Conisbrough Castle as we see it today began in the late 12th century when Isabel and Hamelin de Warenne built a stone tower within an earlier, probably timber, castle. Conisbrough Castle occupies a strategic position on an elevated, natural rock plateau near a ford where a Roman highway crossed the river Don. To the south-west, the castle looks towards the town of Conisbrough, surrounding the eighth-century church of St Peter. To this day, the church tower and the castle's great tower are the most prominent historic landmarks in the area.

The inner bailey was shaped by a ring of earthen banks probably topped with a timber palisade, the defences of the pre-12th-century de Warenne residence. The rubble stone curtain wall was built in about 1200, cutting into the earthen banks. The remains of this wall still encircle the inner bailey.

The medieval castle was probably served by ancillary buildings (such as brewhouses, barns and a smithy) in an outer bailey to the west of the main gate. This area is now occupied by a car park. No evidence has been found to indicate the position of the outer bailey gate, but it might have been in the vicinity of the custodian's lodge, which now houses the visitor centre. The lodge, together with the present gates and boundary wall, was built by the Lane-Fox family in the late 19th century.

Above: The seal impression of John, 7th Earl de Warenne (1240–1304) from about 1250. His shield in the centre bears the chequer pattern of the de Warenne arms

Below: In the Middle Ages Conisbrough Castle overlooked a landscape of woodlands and arable fields which, in later centuries, was populated with collieries, warehouses and housing estates

Facing page: Stairs leading to the second-floor great chamber of the great tower

Above: The approach to the castle from the south-west, looking into the barbican. Enemies attacking the castle would have been funnelled into the narrow curving passage

Below: An illustration of an archer from an English manuscript of about 1325. Archers on the curtain wall and tower would have been able to shoot attackers in the barbican passage below

❶ BARBICAN

On approaching the inner bailey, the curtain wall can be seen to be in a ruined state – the mound visible in the north-west corner of the embankment hides the spoil from excavations in the inner bailey, but possibly also contains remnants of a curtain wall tower that collapsed several hundred years ago.

A path from the visitor centre leads to the barbican – a structure designed to control access to the inner bailey and to hinder enemy attack. The outer bailey would have connected to the barbican by a drawbridge spanning the ditch, which has since been filled in this area to create a flat causeway. The drawbridge was raised in emergencies for additional protection. In many castles, the outer barbican gates were framed by towers, but there is no evidence for such towers at Conisbrough. The narrow barbican passage curves between two parallel walls and becomes a steep climb designed to impede an enemy's progress. A walkway crowning the passage walls was reached via a flight of steps within the barbican passage, and probably gave access to the mechanism which operated the drawbridge.

The north wall of the barbican abuts the plinth of one of the round towers on the curtain wall. This shows that the barbican was built slightly later than the walls and gatehouse, probably in the mid 13th century – a time when castle-builders were developing increasingly complex defensive designs. Similar barbicans can be found in royal residences such as the Tower of London and Newcastle Castle, and the nearby de Warenne castle at Sandal. When Conisbrough was briefly besieged in 1317, however, this elaborate barbican, defended by only a handful of servants, proved ineffective (see page 31).

2 GATEHOUSE

The location of the earliest gatehouse serving the timber castle is unknown. The stone gatehouse was built, together with the curtain wall, in about 1200. It consisted of two round towers either side of a gate passage, with a room above the passage. The gatehouse was substantially remodelled in the 14th century, when its façade was clad in fine-quality ashlar with stone mouldings. The remodelling was perhaps partly paid for by King Edward II (r.1307–27), who, in 1322, spent 40 marks on repairs to the castle's walls and towers.

The eastern gatehouse tower partly collapsed, its masonry slumping down into the castle's ditch, some time before 1538. Although the walls were poorly built with shallow footings, the medieval builders are only partly to blame for the tower's collapse – the unstable geology of the hill also played a role in the disaster. The falling gatehouse tower pulled down the southern stretch of the curtain wall and triggered the ruin of the neighbouring eastward curtain wall tower and adjacent inner bailey buildings. Large fragments of the collapsed gatehouse tower and turret survive in a relatively intact state about 4.5m below their original position.

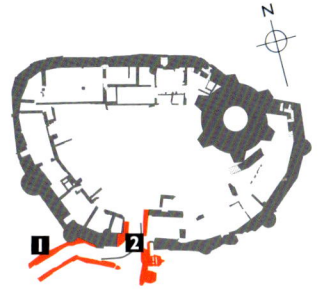

Below: Remains of the east wall of the gatehouse passage. The first-floor doorway connected the room over the gatehouse passage with a building in the south range of the inner bailey: this building might have been a chapel (see page 19)

Left: The remains of the fallen gatehouse tower, with the great tower beyond

A Standing remains of the east wall of the gatehouse

B Masonry of the fallen gatehouse tower

C Slot for a portcullis

D Steps to the barbican wall-walk

E Collapsed south curtain wall

F Great tower

Above: This early 14th-century French manuscript illustration shows a gatehouse with a porter sitting in a niche

Below: The architecture of the entrance doorway of the great tower

A Joggled lintel

B Tympanum

C Relieving arch, spreading the load upon the lintel

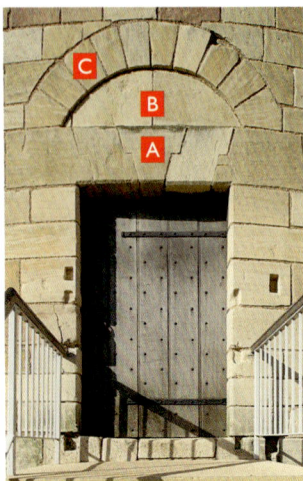

The fallen tower preserves the slot for a portcullis. This heavy grid was lowered across the gate passage from the gatehouse's first-floor chamber, which probably formed part of the accommodation of a porter such as William le Waller, who held the custody of the gate from 18 May 1323 'for life and during good behaviour'. In the employ of King Edward II he was paid two silver pennies a day (the equivalent of two chickens and 24 eggs) and annually a generous one mark (66 pennies) for his 'robe'.

The porter enjoyed the luxury of a heated room – the remains of his fireplace are visible in the western wall of the gatehouse. His chamber also offered access to the upper level of the south range of inner bailey buildings through the door, the jambs of which survive in the stub of the gatehouse's east wall. The porter's job was to control access to the castle, and during the day he would have sat in a small room on one side of the gate or on a bench inside the gate passage, keeping a watchful eye over all who entered or left the castle.

❸ GREAT TOWER

The great tower, at once imposing and graceful, was built by Hamelin de Warenne (c.1129–1202; see page 27) in the 1170s or 1180s. The tower is faced with finely dressed limestone, which was sourced locally. The buttresses emphasized the height and grandeur of the tower while providing fighting platforms at roof level. They are wedge-shaped in plan, wider at the back than at the front, which reduces the splay of the base of the tower and makes it appear taller and slimmer. The buttress to the east of the entrance houses a small chapel at third-floor level: all the others are solid. Perhaps for reasons of expense, the de Warennes did not build other rooms within the buttresses as Hamelin's half-brother, King Henry II (r.1154–89), had done in his contemporary tower at Orford, Suffolk.

The tower entrance would have been reached by a free-standing staircase with a timber drawbridge into the tower, which could perhaps be dismantled for defence. The steep climb would have deterred potential attackers and prepared visitors for the ritual of reception into the lord's great chamber on the second floor of the tower. The joggled lintel (where the notched stones fit together) and tympanum (the semi-circle above the doorway) are made of finely dressed stone. Roman builders used joggled lintels, and the technique was copied by medieval architects in Europe and the Middle East. Norman builders used it in England in ecclesiastical and castle buildings (such as the church of St Lawrence at Hatfield, Herefordshire, and at Chepstow Castle, Monmouthshire). The joggled lintel allowed the builders to span a wide opening with short blocks of stone, and carried associations of sophistication and status. Possibly because of

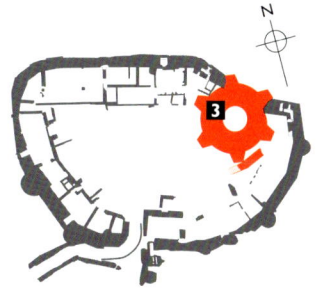

Below: The great tower from the west. A drainage channel in one of the service buildings on the north side of the inner bailey can be seen in the foreground

First floor

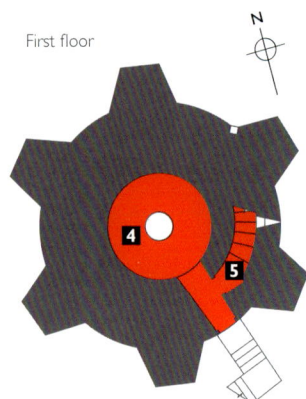

Facing page: Cutaway reconstruction drawing of the great tower in the late 12th century, shortly after it was built

A Entrance staircase

B Access hole to ground-floor chamber and well

C First-floor entrance chamber

D Stairs to second-floor great chamber

E Second-floor great chamber

F Third-floor bedchamber

G Chapel

H Possible arrangement of roof

I Crenellated turret

J Kitchen

Below: Looking out through the great tower's vaulted entrance passage

those associations, it was used by King Henry II's architects at his castles at Orford in Suffolk, Dover in Kent and Tickhill in South Yorkshire. The fireplaces in the gatehouse at Tickhill preserve joggled lintels almost identical to those at Conisbrough. The designer and patron of Conisbrough's great tower might have consciously employed the same technique to enhance the status of the building and to emulate the king.

Admission to the great tower was controlled from the window in the great chamber which overlooked the entrance steps. This window repeats the joggled lintel and tympanum arrangement of the entrance doorway. The entrance is also overlooked by one of the small quadrilobe chapel windows, signifying divine protection to visitors.

4 Ground Floor and First-floor Entrance Chamber

Unusually for an English great tower, the entrance chamber on the first floor has no natural light. With the door closed, and without lamps or torches, the room is plunged into pitch darkness. It is likely, therefore, that this space was used for storage.

The ground-floor chamber beneath the entrance chamber is similarly devoid of windows and has no door. The only access would have been via a ladder through the hole in the centre of its vaulted ceiling. Through this opening, a bucket would have been lowered to draw fresh water from the well immediately below. The ground-floor room was probably also used for storage and maybe even as a strongroom for valuables.

5 Stairs

The arrangement of the stairs within the great tower is highly unusual. English great towers typically have a spiral staircase providing independent access to all floors. At Conisbrough, however, it is only possible to climb to the top of the tower by walking across the chamber on each floor to reach more stairs on the other side.

The stairs leading to the great chamber on the second floor are the most spacious, with wide, well-lit steps. The doorway arch into the great chamber was probably painted, while traces of carving remain on the corner bases at the foot of the jamb. The staircases leading to the upper levels of the great tower are narrower, perhaps reflecting a greater level of privacy. Intriguingly, the remnants of iron fixtures indicate that at every level the doors could only have been locked from outside the chamber. This suggests that an attendant positioned on each staircase would have controlled access to the rooms. Such a curious arrangement might have reflected an intention to restrict movement within the building; its upper floors probably having been open only to a privileged few.

Second floor

N

6 Second-floor Great Chamber

When staying at Conisbrough, the de Warenne lords would have furnished the great chamber with a collection of fine objects and painted furniture, beds with mattresses stuffed with feathers or scented herbs, colourful rugs, silverware and expensive wax candles in enamelled silver holders. The lord could impress important visitors with these lavish items, transforming the cold, stone interior into a luxurious room.

The chimneypiece would have formed a splendid centrepiece with its joggled lintel probably outlined in colour and the hood decorated, as was customary in chambers of such status, with a heraldic shield bearing the yellow and blue de Warenne chequers. The refined foliage carvings of the chimneypiece capitals are similar to examples at York Minster (completed by 1175), and reflected the latest artistic fashion from northern France. Precious wall-hangings, decorated with historical or mythical stories, would have reduced draughts – the windows had internal timber shutters, but no glazing.

To the right of the entrance door is a door leading to the latrine. Next to this is a spacious alcove with a window, which overlooks the entrance to the tower and faced towards Conisbrough's deer park, affording views of the estate.

Above: In the great chamber Earl Hamelin and his guests would have discussed business or enjoyed a private feast in front of the vast fire, as in this 15th century manuscript illustration

Below: Unusually for a 12th-century great tower, the second-floor chamber had its own water basin supplied with running water via lead pipes from rainwater cisterns on the roof

Below right: The enormous fireplace would have been the main decorative feature within the room

Hamelin's Tower

*Although no two medieval great towers are exactly alike, Conisbrough's tower
is unique in its form and architectural iconography.*

In the 12th century, English great towers were typically square or rectangular in plan, with an external staircase sometimes encased in a forebuilding. Conisbrough's tower has a circular core with wedge-shaped buttresses. It was entered via an exposed external staircase, and decorated with architectural details such as joggled lintels and chevron mouldings (see pages 7 and 12). It is similar to a group of circular or polygonal English towers commissioned by Henry II, including Odiham in Hampshire, Chilham in Kent, Tickhill in South Yorkshire and, the most sophisticated, Orford in Suffolk (built 1165–72).

Hamelin de Warenne, Henry II's half-brother, was the only English baron to adopt this new style, building circular towers at Conisbrough, Thorne in South Yorkshire, and at his Normandy estate of Mortemer. Hamelin grew up in the duchy of Anjou and came to England with Henry's court in 1153. As an illegitimate son, Hamelin had neither money nor land and achieved high rank through unwavering loyalty to the king, who arranged his marriage to Isabel de Warenne, one of the richest Norman heiresses. The earldom, gained through this marriage, brought Hamelin vast estates and wealth but in the eyes of many in England he remained a foreign upstart.

Conisbrough was probably the only major de Warenne estate without a stone castle and this offered Hamelin an opportunity to make his mark: his great tower certainly made a powerful statement. Towers in Normandy and Hamelin's native Anjou also tended to be square or oblong. Hamelin, like Henry II at Orford, used an architectural form associated more with their Angevin rivals, the counts of Blois and the kings of France (such as the towers at Provins, Étampes or Châteaudun). This seems surprising, but may have been intended to signify that the Angevins were their equals as members of the ruling class of France, and indeed Europe.

Above: *The circular 12th-century
great tower at Châteaudun, France*
Below: *Henry II's circular great tower
with projecting buttresses at Orford*

Roof

Third floor

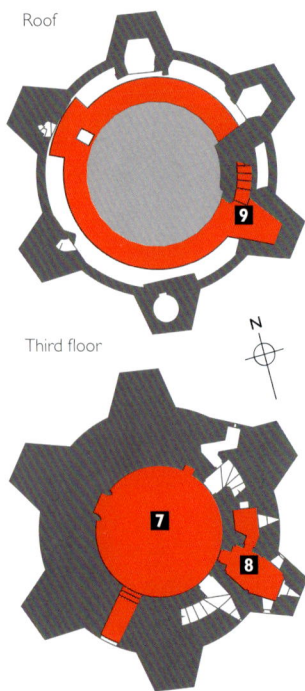

7 Third-floor Bedchamber

Above the great chamber is the bedchamber, where the lord and his family could rest and sleep. This room would have been lavishly decorated and provided with all the available comforts: a sumptuous bed, embroidered cushions, a large basin for washing and a convenient latrine. The room was heated by the fireplace and kept warm with thick wall-hangings and wooden shutters. The fireplace, adorned with intricately carved capitals in the French fashion, gives a hint of its original decoration. The spacious window alcove, which faces towards the town, has stone benches that would have been covered with cushions to provide a place for rest and leisurely pursuits.

8 Chapel

The chapel, which opens off the bedchamber, is formed within one of the buttresses on the eastern side of the tower, to align approximately east to west. The vault had to be carefully contrived to fit the awkward shape of the room. The small quatrefoil windows on either side are the only decorative windows in the tower. The combination of French-style capitals with traditional chevron carving was the height of fashion in the late 12th century, and expressed the taste and wealth of the chapel's patrons. The decoration also helps to date the chapel's construction: around the roof bosses and on the chevrons of the east window are leaf carvings similar to examples on the choir vault ribs at York Minster, built in about 1175.

In this chapel, Isabel and Hamelin de Warenne and their closest family and household would have attended Mass in private. In 1180–89 Isabel and Hamelin endowed a chapel within the castle, dedicated to Saints Philip and James, with the income from their mills in Conisbrough. This money paid for a priest to pray for their souls and those of their fathers, as well as for Henry II. It is likely that this endowment was for this private chapel in the great tower. The priest would have lived at the castle praying even in the absence of the lord and lady – a constant reminder of their ownership of the castle. The

Above: This 15th-century manuscript illustration shows a bedchamber with luxurious furnishings. The de Warenne earls would have brought such items with them when they travelled between their estates, making the bare rooms of the great tower comfortable during their stay

Below: The fireplace with its joggled lintel and richly carved capitals would have heated the third-floor chamber

Left: *The interior of the chapel. The basin (piscina) is one of two on opposite sides of the chapel – an unusual arrangement, as normally the two basins would be side-by-side. Double piscinas were introduced in the late 12th century*
Above: *Illustration of about 1325 showing a lady praying and a priest celebrating Mass*
Below: *A medieval bodkin arrowhead and a tiny cluster of chain mail, excavated at Conisbrough, and perhaps used by the castle's guards*

priest's vestments and vessels were kept in the sacristy which opens off the chapel, and the two piscinas (basins) were used for washing the priest's hands and the altar vessels before and after the Mass.

9 Roof

The roof originally looked very different from how it appears today. Evidence for its structure is slight, but it is likely that the vaulted stairs from the bedchamber led to a circular passage at the present parapet walkway level, which offered access to a room in the centre, directly above the bedchamber, and which was crowned with a conical roof.

Small spaces inside the buttresses performed various functions. The one next to the entrance steps, which has T-shaped sockets to house external timber platforms, called hoardings, was designed for defensive and practical purposes, such as hoisting supplies. Other spaces functioned as water cisterns, which provided rainwater via pipes to the basins in the rooms beneath, and one housed a bread oven. The buttresses probably rose much higher than at present to form crenellated turrets, two of which contained staircases leading to an upper parapet level from where guards could survey the town and surrounding landscape.

INNER BAILEY

In the Middle Ages, the inner bailey would have been a bustling place crowded with buildings. The first Earl de Warenne must have erected some timber buildings here in the late 11th century, and his successors altered and expanded them to suit their needs. Archaeological excavations in the inner bailey in the 1960s and 1970s revealed the footings of stone buildings that can still be seen, as well as many fragments of carved stones. These suggest that the timber buildings were rebuilt in stone when the stone curtain wall was erected in about 1200.

⑩ CURTAIN WALL

In contrast to the finely jointed ashlar of the great tower, the curtain wall is poorly built of roughly dressed coursed stone with ashlar quoins (corner stones) concealing a rubble core. This rubble core was exposed in places when the inner bailey buildings were demolished, and in others when the stone was robbed out. The semicircular towers are solid and have no internal chambers – a design introduced by architects working for King John (r.1199–1216) in early 13th-century castles at Knaresborough and Scarborough. The awkward way in which the curtain wall abuts the great tower confirms that it was the product of a secondary, slightly later building campaign.

In two short sections – one on the north and one on the west side – the roughly coursed exterior stone facing of the curtain wall has been replaced with stretches of finely squared ashlar. These may be remnants of works carried out in the 14th century, perhaps by the last Earl de Warenne or by Edmund of Langley, who owned the castle after 1347, but the quality of the ashlar is similar to the great tower, and the stones may have come from a 12th-century building. Walkways along the top of the curtain wall allowed defenders to survey the surrounding landscape.

⑪ KITCHEN

With limited space in the inner bailey, the service buildings on the north side crowded close to the great tower. The kitchen was originally a timber-framed, square, detached building, probably with a pyramidal roof and central hearth – a typical medieval arrangement. It was later enlarged and linked to the

Top: A late 12th-century capital excavated within the inner bailey. It is of the same style, date and quality as the decoration of the great tower. This, and other similar pieces found at Conisbrough, suggests that Hamelin built at least one other high-status stone building in the inner bailey
Above: The exterior of the curtain wall on the west side of the inner bailey. A short stretch of the finer 14th-century cladding can be seen to the left

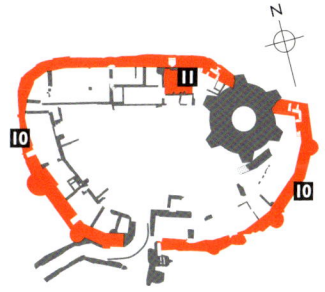

Left: The medieval kitchen

A Location of central hearth

B Wall fireplaces

C Oven

D Post-medieval stone robbing

E Service buildings

F Corbels supporting roof structure

other service rooms on this side of the inner bailey, forming a single range with the great hall. The central hearth was replaced by fireplaces in the walls; the relics of these and their stone hearths can be seen on the north and east sides, and when lit in preparation for a feast, the heat must have been oppressive. A drainage channel leading to the external ditch can be seen to the east of the kitchen walls running towards the curtain wall. The service range had its own latrine to the east of the kitchen within the curtain wall.

All the supplies for a grand medieval feast – such as venison, poultry, fish, flour, sugar and spices, as well as wine and ale – were stored in a larder. The buildings between the kitchen and great hall might have been a pantry (from *pain*, the French word for bread) and buttery (from *botte*, French for a barrel), from where food would have been served during a feast. These service buildings had two storeys; the rooms on the upper floor would have provided accommodation and possibly given access to a minstrels' gallery over the service passage at the east end of the hall. The service range was probably originally connected to the great hall by an open walkway with a pentice roof: 13th-century accounts record the nails bought to build the 'pales' (or fencing) between the kitchen and the hall. This walkway was later enclosed to form a corridor.

Below: This illustration from a mid 14th-century manuscript gives a sense of the heat and activity in a castle's medieval kitchen

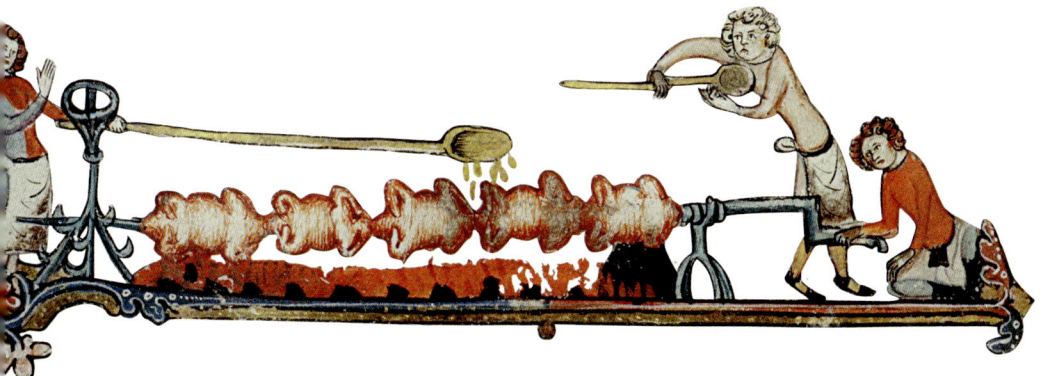

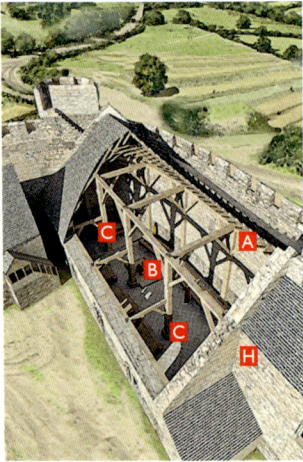

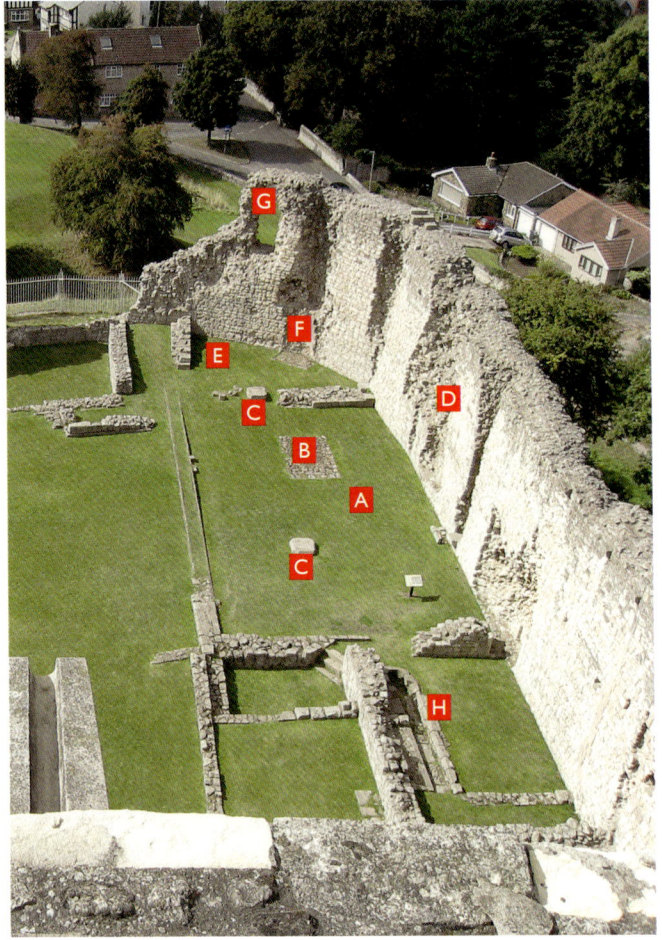

Above right: Remains of the great hall and later solar

Above: Reconstructions showing the great hall in about 1200 (top) and in the 14th century, following the insertion of the solar block at the western end (below)

A Great hall

B Central hearth

C Stone plinths which supported the aisle posts

D Probable location of 14th-century fireplace

E Solar

F Solar fireplace

G Door to garderobe

H Service buildings

🔢 GREAT HALL

The great hall was the largest room in the castle. Here, the lord and lady dined not only with important guests, but also with their entire household, as well as tenants and visitors of all ranks.

Before the inner bailey buildings were rebuilt in stone, there would have been a timber hall somewhere within the inner bailey. In about 1200, when the stone curtain wall was added, a new great hall was built on the north side of the inner bailey, extending into the north-west corner. This hall had a single aisle of four bays on the south side. Two of the three stone plinths for the timber aisle posts survive *in situ*. The posts formed an arcade which supported the roof. Opposite each aisle post was another timber post set against, or partly within the thickness of, the curtain wall. Some of the stone pads for these posts are still visible towards the base of the curtain wall. The central hearth, a traditional feature of early Norman halls, lies awkwardly close to where the missing aisle post plinth would have stood and may be a relic of an earlier building.

In the 14th century, a two-storey solar block was inserted into the west end of the great hall. The central hearth was probably buried at this time when the floor level within the hall was raised. A new fireplace was inserted into the curtain wall.

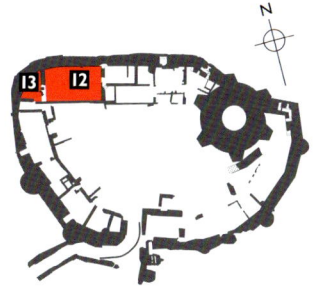

The seating arrangement in a medieval hall reflected the household's hierarchy: the lord and lady and their important guests sat at the high table, which is so-called because it stood on a raised platform (dais) at the west end of the hall. The lower status members of the household sat beneath them at long tables arranged along the sides of the hall.

Many lavish banquets were held at Conisbrough, such as the extravagant feast presided over by Thomas of Lancaster in 1319, which lasted for two days and cost 15 shillings – the equivalent of three years' rent for a small cottage. The courts of the Honour of Conisbrough (an estate comprising many villages on the eastern edge of South Yorkshire) were held in the great hall, with the earl or his steward judging minor offences, such as theft, trespass, assault and land disputes.

13 SOLAR

In the later Middle Ages, castle owners often chose to live in more comfortable accommodation within the inner bailey rather than in the chambers of great towers. The lord's private rooms (the solar) were usually built adjacent to the high end of the great hall. The two-storey solar block at Conisbrough was inserted into the west end of the great hall probably in the 14th century. The remains of the ground-floor fireplace can still be seen, and there may have been another on the floor above. The large opening at first-floor level was the doorway to a latrine. Part of the round arch which supported the outer face of the latrine survives in the external face of the wall.

When Countess Maud Clifford lived at Conisbrough (from 1415 to 1446) she filled her private rooms with luxurious furnishings (see page 34). Her bedroom on the upper floor of the solar would have been more comfortable than the cold rooms of the great tower, and reflected the castle's new role as the permanent residence of a great noblewoman.

Below: A fragment of late medieval coloured window glass set in lead, excavated at Conisbrough. The glass probably came from the high-status rooms of the solar

Bottom: Manuscript illustration of the 15th century showing a lady dining in a great hall. Another table is arranged along the side of the room and expensive items of plate, like those described in Maud Clifford's will (see page 34), are displayed on a dresser

'[The hall is] a common habitation of men, the receptacle of eaters and drinkers, conversing frivolously, scurrilously, and perhaps often filthily, and perhaps sometimes even acting filthily, with dogs also running about it, and sleeping and often leaving their dirt there.'
Robert Grosseteste, Bishop of Lincoln, describing William, 6th Earl de Warenne's hall at Grantham in about 1232–40

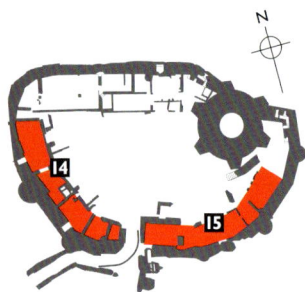

Below: This 14th-century jug, made in a kiln just two miles from the castle, was excavated intact from the bottom of the latrine chute in the centre of the apartment range

Bottom: The basement room on the south side of the inner bailey, adjacent to the gate, might have been a prison cell, equipped with a latrine

14 APARTMENTS

The solar adjoined the northern end of a range of buildings on the west side of the inner bailey. Excavations in the 1960s and 1970s recovered many small toiletry articles from this part of the inner bailey, indicating that these buildings housed domestic apartments. The excavations also revealed that this range was built in the 13th century and remodelled in the 14th and 15th centuries. The buildings had two storeys, and the timber roofs of the upper chambers rested on the stone corbels that still survive in the upper part of the curtain wall. The scar of a fireplace and flue at first-floor level shows that the rooms were probably heated, but the level of comfort varied – high-ranking servants and important guests would have occupied the better apartments on the upper floor. The L-shaped area in the middle of the range incorporates a deep chute marking the location of a latrine. The chute was altered several times – at some point between the 13th and 15th century a blocking wall and a sharply pointed arch, built of reused masonry, were inserted, probably to improve the amenities and structural integrity of the building.

In the south-west corner of the inner bailey, adjacent to the gate, is a small basement room with a flagstone floor and a latrine seat against the curtain wall. Because of its proximity to

Left: View of the inner bailey from the roof of the great tower, looking west over the town of Conisbrough

A Great hall

B Solar block

C Apartments

D Fireplace

E Latrine chute

F Corbels supporting roofs of first-floor rooms

G Lodge building (housing the visitor centre)

H St Peter's Church

the gatehouse, it could have been used by the castle's guards or functioned as a prison cell. Documents show that prisoners were sometimes held at the castle; for example, some time before 1326, an influential royal official, Robert de Morton, raided the land of one Alexander Martyn from Hatfield, near Doncaster, and imprisoned him at Conisbrough for a week.

15 SOUTH RANGE

A substantial range of outbuildings once existed in the south-east corner of the inner bailey. There is no evidence as to their function, except for the building aligned east to west and connected to the gatehouse. Excavations of the collapsed curtain wall revealed a piscina belonging to this building. An altar slab, now in St Peter's Church, Conisbrough (see page 21), was found in this area in the 1920s. These suggest that this building was one of the castle chapels. Perhaps the timber delivered for repairs to a chapel roof, mentioned in the 1317–22 accounts of Thomas of Lancaster, was for this building.

The remaining door at the upper level shows that it was a double-storey building. In the 14th century a latrine chamber was inserted here, and its remains are preserved within the collapsed wall. The upper storey might have provided accommodation for the priest.

Below: The collapsed masonry of the south side of the curtain wall. The passage which led to a latrine can be seen in the foreground

Above: 12th-century window glass, now located in the windows of the north aisle, includes figures from the Old Testament, including this depiction of Moses

Right: The nave of St Peter's church, looking east

A Blocked Anglo-Saxon window

B Chancel

C Blocked Anglo-Saxon window

D Blocked Anglo-Saxon window into *porticus*

E 15th-century windows

F Norman arcades

Below: Reconstruction drawings showing how St Peter's Church might have looked in about 1000 (**A**) and in about 1200, following 12th-century alterations (**B**)

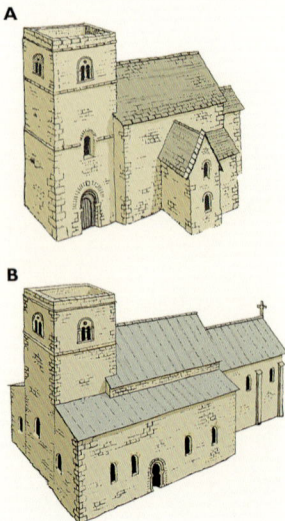

The Church of St Peter

At first glance, the church of St Peter, which stands in the centre of Conisbrough, appears to be a typical late medieval parish church, but its fabric preserves the remains of the oldest building in South Yorkshire.

An Anglo-Saxon Foundation

Conisbrough might have been the location of one of 12 'minsters' which King Oswy of Northumbria (r.642–70) founded to celebrate his victory over the Mercian King Penda (r.c.626–655) in 635, the event which supposedly led to Oswy's conversion to Christianity. Like many of the earliest Anglo-Saxon monastic churches, Conisbrough was probably associated with a royal estate, and served several towns across an area that stretched from Hatfield Chase, a low-lying area east of Doncaster, to Harthill on the southern border of Yorkshire.

Several of the earliest Anglo-Saxon churches were dedicated to St Peter, so this dedication, as well as its proportions and the manner of its construction, suggest that it was probably built in the mid eighth century. Its long, rectangular nave is typical of 'Northumbrian' style churches of this date. The nave preserves massive quoins arranged in a typical Anglo-Saxon pattern, and blocked Anglo-Saxon windows can be seen in the nave walls above the later Norman arcades. Above the middle nave arch on the north side, a blocked round-headed window opens into the nave from a chamber (now gone) to the north. This side chamber was probably a *porticus* – a characteristic feature of early medieval church architecture, which may have been used for a variety of liturgical or funerary functions.

The original chancel was enlarged in about 1050 and extended eastwards in the 15th century, but the outline of its roof can still be seen on the east face of the chancel arch. The lower parts of the tower may not be contemporary with the nave, but probably predate the Norman Conquest of 1066.

Medieval Expansion

The Anglo-Saxon church proved too small for the medieval town of Conisbrough, which flourished under the Norman de Warenne earls of Surrey. The Norman lords enlarged the chancel and added the side aisles, knocking arches through the walls of the Anglo-Saxon nave.

Several of the church's 12th-century windows, depicting characters from the Old Testament, were incorporated into the north aisle during its Victorian

remodelling. An altar slab, said to come from the castle chapel and dating probably to the early 13th century, is now kept in the north presbytery chapel.

The Late Medieval Church

In the 14th and 15th centuries links with Conisbrough Castle remained strong and the castle's owners continued to make their mark on the church. The south aisle was rebuilt, the tower re-faced and a new porch built. Pieces of 15th-century stained glass survive in the south windows of the chancel and include depictions of the Virgin and a male figure identified as Prior Atwell of Lewes Priory, Sussex, which was founded by William I de Warenne (see page 25).

Several people connected with the castle were buried in the church. Among them was one of Countess Maud Clifford's lady companions, Katherine Fitzwilliam (née Welles) whose memorial bore her heraldic device, and another of William Amias, a Tudor deputy steward of the Honour of Tickhill and Conisbrough. Unfortunately, their memorials can no longer be found.

Above: Fragments of 15th-century window glass, now incorporated into windows of the south wall of the chancel, include depictions of Prior Atwell of Lewes (top left) and a bishop (centre) – probably Saint Blaise, patron saint of wool combers

Below: Two early stone grave covers now stand in the east end of the south aisle. One, believed to be Saxon, is decorated with carvings of birds, which may represent ravens and refer to the ancient local Raven family. The other, below, is thought to be Norman and depicts a contest between a knight and a dragon

History of the Castle

BEFORE THE CASTLE

People have been living in the area around Conisbrough since prehistoric times, and coins and pottery discovered around the town indicate that there was a Roman settlement here some time between the first and fourth centuries.

The name Conisbrough, however, derives from the Anglo-Saxon 'Cyninges-burh', meaning 'the king's borough'. It is not known for certain who the king in question was, but there is a strong possibility that its origins go back to the seventh or eighth century, and that the name refers to one of the Anglian kings of Northumbria. Anglo-Saxon pottery found on the castle hill, and the age of the town's parish church support this argument. The church, dedicated to St Peter, began as a Saxon building of the seventh or eighth century (see page 20), and, despite many later alterations, it is the oldest building in South Yorkshire.

In the years immediately before the Norman Conquest of 1066, Conisbrough was located at the centre of a large estate which covered much of the south-east corner of Yorkshire. It was owned by Earl Harold Godwinson, who seized the English throne after the death of Edward the Confessor (r.1042–66) in 1066. Harold went on to fight William, Duke of Normandy, later William I (r.1066–87) at the Battle of Hastings that year, where he lost both the Crown and his life.

Above: Fragments of Anglo-Saxon pottery found on the castle hill show that the area was occupied from as early as the eighth century
Below: Ambrosius Aurelius pursues Hengist at the gates of Conisbrough Castle in this illustration from a 14th-century copy of the poet Wace's Roman de Brut, *which was based on Geoffrey of Monmouth's tale*

Facing page: 19th-century depiction of Conisbrough's great tower, before restoration of the roof and upper floors

The Mythic History of Conisbrough

By the 12th century, Conisbrough had an alternative, mythic history. The 12th-century cleric and historian Geoffrey of Monmouth wrote in his *Historia Regum Britanniae* ('History of the Kings of Britain') that a British leader, Conan, founded a stronghold called 'Conan's burg'. This was later granted to a Saxon leader, Hengist, who initially served the British king Vortigern as a mercenary.

When hostilities broke out between the Britons and the Saxons, another British leader, Ambrosius Aurelius, defeated Hengist at the Battle of 'Maisbeli'. According to Geoffrey of Monmouth's tale, Hengist was captured and beheaded, and buried at the entrance to 'Cunengeburg', that is, Conisbrough.

There is no evidence to link the shadowy historical figure Hengist to Conisbrough or to support this account. Geoffrey might have created this ancient and dramatic story

about the castle as a compliment to Conisbrough's owners at the time, the de Warennes. Until the 18th century, however, this account was accepted as fact.

Above: Section of the Bayeux Tapestry showing Norman knights at the Battle of Hastings
Below: Engraving of the tomb slab of Gundrada de Warenne, who died in 1085, now in Southover church, Sussex

WILLIAM DE WARENNE'S CASTLE

From the late 11th century until 1347 Conisbrough belonged to the de Warenne family, one of the great dynasties of medieval England. They took their name from the valley of the river Varenne, south of Dieppe on the eastern border of Normandy. The family can be traced back to Ralph I de Warenne, who owned land in Rouen in 1030. In 1066 his younger son, William I de Warenne (d.1088), was among the leaders of the Norman expedition to conquer England. He was present at the Battle of Hastings, and after the Norman victory he was given land in 13 English counties, including the Honour of Conisbrough – a compact block of about 28 villages covering much of the eastern edge of South Yorkshire. He was one of William the Conqueror's closest associates, and was among those left in charge of England when the king returned to Normandy in 1067. William I de Warenne probably established a residence at Conisbrough and visited it annually.

William's wife Gundrada died in childbirth on 27 May 1085. Her husband served William I and his son William II Rufus (r.1087–1100) loyally. In the spring of 1088 he helped William II suppress a rebellion led by Odo, Bishop of Bayeux, and about this time the king made him Earl of Surrey, with the additional title of Earl de Warenne. Earl William died soon after this, probably in June 1088, and was buried with Gundrada in the chapter house of Lewes Priory, Sussex. Their son William succeeded as the 2nd earl (d.1138). He too served the Crown loyally, fighting for Henry I (r.1100–35) in the Battle of Tinchebrai (1106), and was given the manor of Wakefield in 1121. He married Elizabeth of Vermandois, and

The Lewes Cartulary

In 1077 William I de Warenne and his wife Gundrada made a pilgrimage to Rome. On the way they stopped at the great abbey of Cluny in Burgundy, and were so impressed by what they saw that they asked its abbot to provide them with monks to found a Cluniac priory at Lewes, on their estates in Sussex. The first monks arrived at Lewes the next year and William and Gundrada supervised the construction of an enormous monastery, the first Cluniac house in England. William and Gundrada gave all the churches on their Yorkshire estates, including that at Conisbrough, to the new priory. Lewes Priory's cartulary, recording all the grants it received, is the main documentary source for the history of Conisbrough and its castle in the 11th and 12th centuries.

assumed her family's coat of arms, a chequer pattern of blue and yellow: this became famous as the 'Warenne chequer'. He was succeeded by his son, another William (1119–48), who became the 3rd earl. The 3rd earl was a member of the elite royal guard of Louis VII of France and was killed defending Louis during fighting in Turkey while on the Second Crusade in 1148, leaving his daughter, Isabel, as the greatest heiress in England.

We know very little of the castle in these years. The inner bailey was apparently surrounded by earth banks, which probably supported timber palisades. There would have been timber buildings inside the bailey, including in all likelihood a hall, a chamber and a kitchen, and there was probably an outer bailey also built of timber.

Above: Cluny Abbey in Burgundy, as depicted in a 12th-century manuscript illustration. William I de Warenne was inspired to found the first Cluniac priory in England on his estate at Lewes, Sussex, after visiting the abbey

Left: Before the construction of the stone curtain wall at Conisbrough Castle, the earth banks of the inner bailey were probably topped by a timber palisade

The de Warenne Estates

The de Warennes retained large estates on the eastern fringe of Normandy, but after the Norman Conquest in 1066 they were given even larger estates in England.

The de Warennes maintained their principle residence at their Lewes estate and were buried in the chapter house of the priory there. Impressive remains of Lewes Castle survive today, but only fragments of the great priory.

The de Warennes also owned lands in the eastern part of Surrey around Reigate, where they had another major castle, and great estates in East Anglia, run from Castle Acre in Norfolk, where they built a castle and laid out a town next to it. In 1085 they founded a second Cluniac priory at Castle Acre; impressive remains of both the castle and the priory survive today. The family also had estates in Bedfordshire, Buckinghamshire, Hampshire, Cambridgeshire, Lincolnshire, Huntingdonshire, and Oxfordshire, as well as the Honour of Conisbrough in Yorkshire, which included land in Fishlake, Harthill, Kirk Sandall and Thorne, and important fisheries at Hatfield. To this, Henry I added the large manor of Wakefield, in about 1121.

A 12th-century document in Lewes Priory's cartulary records that the people who lived near the river Wellstream in the Fenlands, south of the Wash, had an annual obligation to help Earl Hamelin and Countess Isabel cross this treacherous tidal river when travelling to and from Yorkshire, suggesting that they maintained a residence at Conisbrough and visited it annually.

Above: The ruins of Lewes Castle, Sussex. A motte and bailey castle was built here soon after the Norman Conquest, by William I de Warenne (see page 24)
Left: The inner bailey of Castle Acre Castle, Norfolk

ISABEL DE WARENNE AND HAMELIN OF ANJOU

Isabel de Warenne (c.1130–1203) inherited her father's vast estates in 1148. The marriage of such a great heiress was a matter for the king to decide, and King Stephen (r.1135–54) married her to his younger son, William (c.1137–59), who, through her, became 4th Earl de Warenne and Earl of Surrey. King Stephen's reign was a turbulent time: he had seized the throne, although his cousin Matilda, daughter of the previous king, Henry I, arguably had a better claim to it. After many years of civil war, Stephen signed the treaty of Westminster, which agreed that Matilda's son Henry, Count of Anjou, would succeed to the throne, rather than either of his own sons. William's position and estates were guaranteed under the treaty. In the event, William and Isabel's marriage was childless: when he died in 1159 the Warenne estates reverted to her, and she held them directly for five years.

By this time, Matilda's son Henry had succeeded to the throne as Henry II. For a second time, Isabel's marriage was decided by the king: this time to Henry II's illegitimate half-brother Hamelin of Anjou. We know nothing about Hamelin's mother or his earlier life, and it is a measure of how important Isabel's family was that, when they married, he adopted her name and her family's coat of arms, as well as its titles, succeeding as 5th Earl de Warenne and Earl of Surrey. By the late 12th century the Warenne estates were reckoned at about 140 knights' fees, meaning that they owed the Crown the service of 140 knights. The standard term of service was 40 days a year, though by this date the service was normally commuted to a money payment, called scutage. In 1173 Hamelin was the ninth greatest lord in England, as reckoned by this measure. He remained loyal to his half-brother, supporting Henry II in all the crises of his reign.

Conisbrough Rebuilt

Hamelin and Isabel probably travelled around their great estates each year. Lewes remained their principal residence, but they certainly visited Conisbrough, where a steward, Otes de Tilly, lived and looked after their estates. It was probably Hamelin and Isabel who began rebuilding the castle in stone.

Above: Henry II seated on his throne, from a late 13th-century manuscript
Below: Hamelin and Isabel de Warenne would have travelled between their estates, spending time at each and taking their valuable possessions with them. This illustration from an English manuscript of about 1325 shows a royal lady travelling in a sumptuous carriage

Above: Conisbrough Castle from the south-west. The curtain wall was probably built shortly after the great tower

Below: Depiction of the coronation of Richard I (r.1189–99) from a manuscript of about 1250

We have no documentary evidence for its construction, but architectural details in the great tower closely resemble features at York Minster, suggesting that it was built in the 1170s or 1180s to provide relatively private accommodation, and as an expression of Isabel and Hamelin's wealth and status. It is not certain if they also built the curtain wall around the inner bailey, though it seems likely to have been added a little later, in a second phase of building work (see page 14).

Little is known of Hamelin and Isabel personally. Hamelin only bore witness to ten known charters of Henry II suggesting that, despite his kinship with the king and his loyalty, he was not in Henry's inner circle. He witnessed 13 of the charters of Richard I, however, and when Richard departed on Crusade, Hamelin was one of the most prominent loyalists, opposing the conspiracies of Richard's brother, Prince John. Hamelin's last major public role was to carry the sword of state at Richard's second coronation in 1194, after the king's return to England. Hamelin died on 7 May 1202, and Isabel shortly after: they, too, were buried in the chapter house of Lewes Priory, the mausoleum of the de Warennes. Their son William de Warenne (d.1240) succeeded as 6th earl. Their daughters Isabella and Ela married into neighbouring knightly families in Yorkshire, and their daughter Maud married twice, to great French lords. These marriages reveal the breadth of the family's interests and social connections.

THE LATER DE WARENNE EARLS

Soon after William had succeeded as 6th earl, the family lost their Norman estates when Philip Augustus of France captured the duchy of Normandy from King John in 1204–5. Earl William remained loyal to the Crown: it is possible that it was he who added the curtain wall and towers around the inner bailey, in response to the troubled times of John's reign. The curtain wall was lined with stone buildings, including a hall, kitchen, service buildings and apartments, remains of which can be seen today. In 1215 William married Maud, daughter of William Marshal, Earl of Pembroke, a celebrated warrior and leader of the regency government in the first years of the reign of the young King Henry III (r.1216–72), who came to the throne aged nine.

Below: A fragment of painted wall plaster (right) and a mason's iron chisel (left), found at Conisbrough. The inner bailey buildings were replaced in stone at the beginning of the 13th century

'Diabolical' Oppressions

John, 7th Earl de Warenne (1231–1304), and his representatives ruthlessly enforced their authority over the local population of Conisbrough.

In the Middle Ages legal authority was divided between the king and his representatives, the Church, and the local lord and his agents – a complicated arrangement that often led to confusion and trouble. In 1277, John, 7th Earl de Warenne, claimed many rights over his South Yorkshire estates: the right to carry out judgments involving the death sentence; the right to regulate the price and quality of bread and beer; the regulation of weights and measures; the right to settle disputes where blood had been shed, and the right to judge cases where landlords seized goods in lieu of unpaid rent. In practice, the earl was rarely there. This gave his agents, who exercised power on his behalf and had armed men at their disposal, considerable scope for making money dishonestly.

In 1277 the local people were forced to appeal to the king's officials against the earl's steward, Richard de Heydon. Among other 'innumerable and diabolical' oppressions, he had unlawfully imprisoned Beatrice, wife of William the Taylor of Rotherham, for a year. The earl's constable, Nigel Drury, also seems to have been unscrupulous: he stole six stone of wool from one townsman of Conisbrough and a horse with a sackful of oats from another, and took them to the castle.

The earl seems to have claimed that they were taken in lieu of unpaid rent. As royal authority carried some weight during the reign of Edward I (1272–1307), the townsfolk might well have obtained justice on this occasion.

Below: A 15th-century manuscript illustration showing the collection of taxes. Earl John and his agents were accused of levying arbitrary taxes, fines and tolls and wrongfully imprisoning local inhabitants

After the 6th earl's death in 1239, Conisbrough was entrusted to Countess Maud on behalf of her son John, the 7th earl, then aged only nine. The castle was occupied by the de Warennes periodically in the 13th century.

John, the 7th earl, was a strict and unpopular landlord. His aggressive temperament brought him into conflict with the nearest great dynasty, the de Lacy lords of Pontefract: Henry III had to prevent them from coming to blows over a land dispute in 1268. The 7th earl's steward, Richard de Heydon, became notorious in South Yorkshire for his harsh exactions against the estate's tenants, while Nigel Drury, his constable of Conisbrough, was equally unpopular.

Earl John's son and heir William was killed in a tournament at Croydon on 15 December 1286, and when John died in 1304, he was succeeded by his grandson, another John, the 8th and last Earl de Warenne, who was then aged about 18.

THE LAST EARL DE WARENNE

John, 8th Earl de Warenne (1286–1347) had a chequered and turbulent life. Edward I married the young earl to Joan de Bar, Edward's granddaughter. It was a mark of royal favour, but the marriage was not a happy one, and was childless. Both husband and wife asked for a divorce in 1314, but were refused one by the Church. They then lived apart, the earl living with his mistress, Maud de Nerford, with whom he had several children.

Earl John became embroiled in a feud with the most powerful man in England after the king: Thomas, Earl of Lancaster, who was married to Alice de Lacy, heiress to the

Abduction of Alice de Lacy

'The Countess of Lancaster … was seized at Canford, in Dorset, by a certain knight of the house and family of John, Earl Warenne, with many English retainers called together for the detestable deed, as it is said, with the royal assent. … With them was a certain man of miserable stature, lame and hunchbacked, called Richard de St Martin, exhibiting and declaring constantly his evil intentions towards the lady, so miserably led away.'
Thomas Walsingham, *Historia Anglicana*, late 14th century

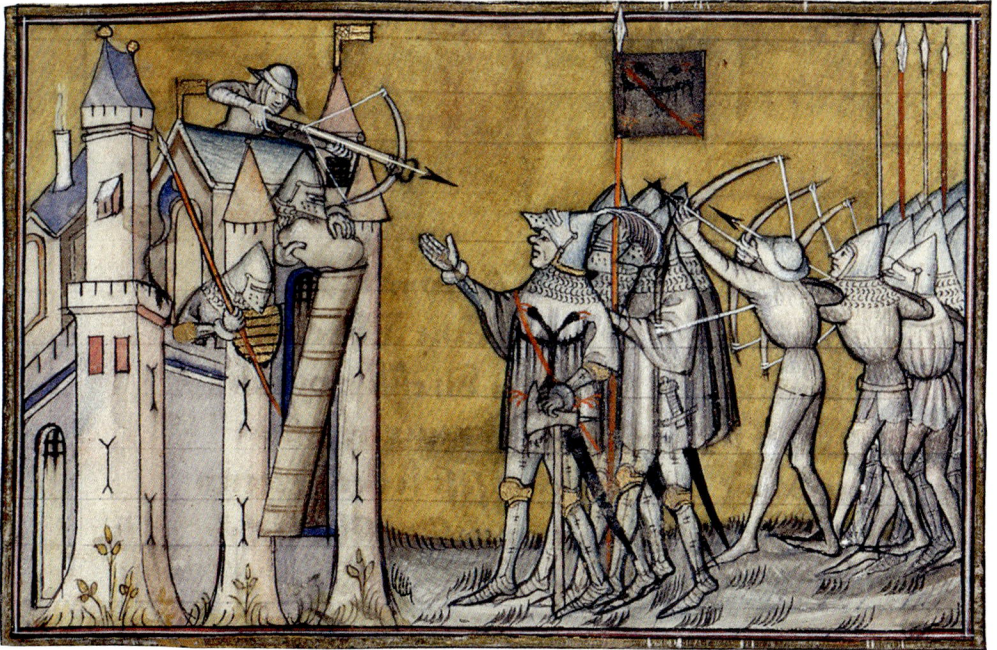

nearby lordship of Pontefract. In 1317, for reasons which
remain obscure, Earl John kidnapped Alice de Lacy at Canford
in Dorset and imprisoned her at Reigate Castle, Surrey.
Earl Thomas suspected his wife of infidelity with Earl John
and obtained a divorce. He sent forces to seize the de
Warenne estates in Yorkshire, including their castles at Sandal
and Conisbrough.

Thomas of Lancaster's men found the gates of
Conisbrough Castle shut, but they assaulted it unopposed and
discovered just six men inside, including the town's miller and
three brothers, Thomas, Henry and William Greathead,
men-at-arms. Earl John did not have the means to regain his
Yorkshire estates, and surrendered them to Earl Thomas in
1319 in return for property in Somerset and Wiltshire worth
1,000 marks (£666 6s. 8d.) a year. Thomas of Lancaster
installed a constable at Conisbrough and carried out repairs.

Thomas would doubtless have retained the de Warennes'
Yorkshire estates had he not openly rebelled against Edward II,
been defeated at the Battle of Boroughbridge in March 1322,
and executed. His estates were seized and the Honour of
Conisbrough was eventually returned to Earl John in 1328, by
Edward III (r.1327–77). The episode remains mysterious,
though Earl John seems to have borne a grudge against
Thomas of Lancaster for blocking his divorce. It is also possible
that Earl John acted with royal encouragement.

The 8th earl's mistress, Maud de Nerford, and both their
sons died before him, so the Warenne line came to an end at
his death in 1347, and the estates reverted to the Crown.
Edward III gave the Yorkshire de Warenne estates to his
fourth son Edmund of Langley (1341–1402), who had been
the 8th earl de Warenne's godson.

Above: Late 14th-century manuscript
illustration of a castle under attack.
Thomas of Lancaster's men found
Conisbrough poorly defended when
they took the castle in 1317
Below: The execution of Thomas
of Lancaster in 1322, depicted in
a near-contemporary manuscript
of 1325

Right: Reconstruction of Conisbrough
Castle in about 1440, looking north

A Inner bailey

B Great tower

C Kitchen

D Great hall

E Solar block

F Apartments

G Gatehouse

H South range

I Barbican

J Outer bailey

K River Don

Below: Late 14th-century gilt-bronze
statuette of Edmund of Langley,
Duke of York, from the tomb of
his father, King Edward III, in
Westminster Abbey

THE HOUSE OF YORK

From 1347 Conisbrough belonged to Edmund of Langley and
his descendants, of the House of York, who played a major
role in the turbulent history of England in the later 14th and
15th centuries. Edmund was created Earl of Cambridge by his
father Edward III and, in 1385, was made Duke of York by his
nephew Richard II (r.1377–99). His main seat was at
Fotheringhay in Northamptonshire, but Conisbrough was an
important secondary residence: as such, it was more often
used by the House of York than it had been by the de
Warennes. Major additions made to the domestic buildings in
the castle some time in the 14th century were more probably
carried out under the House of York than under the last de
Warenne earl. Edmund employed a parker named Henry
de Westby at Conisbrough, who would have fed the deer,
protected them from poachers, and maintained the boundary
of Conisbrough's deer park, which lay to the south of the castle.

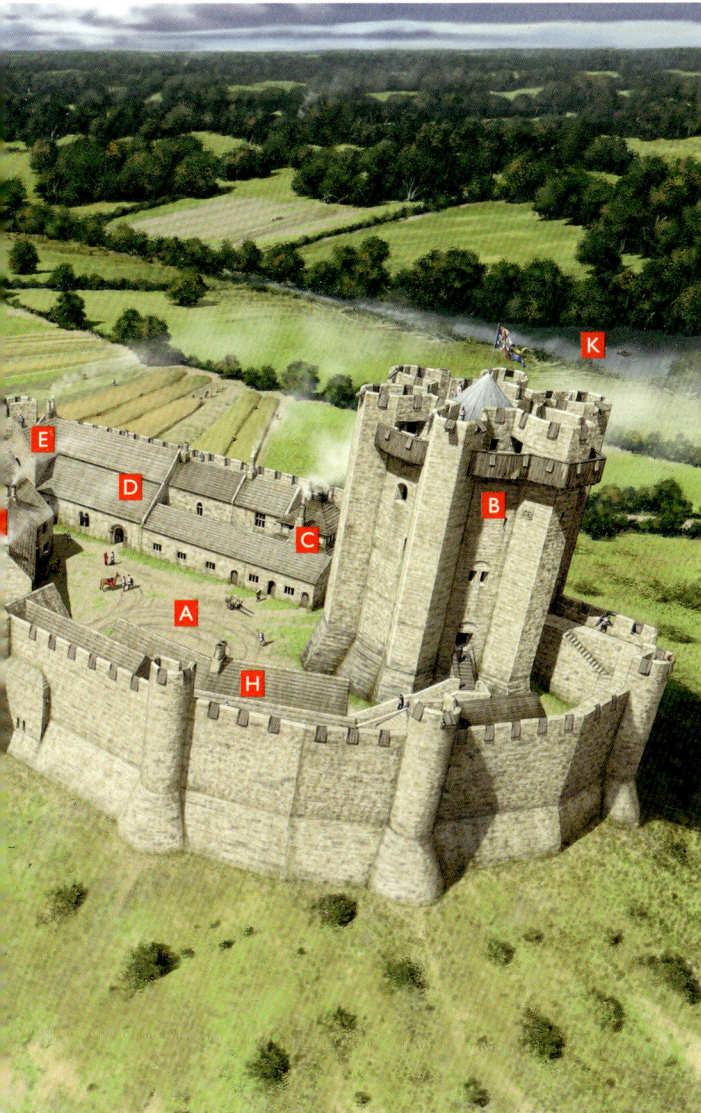

Below: *A hunting arrowhead and a butchered antler from a fallow deer, both excavated at the castle. Conisbrough's deer park, looked after in the 14th century by parker Henry de Westby, would have provided venison for the lord's table*

Bottom: *A 15th-century manuscript illustration of the coronation of King Henry IV, 1399*

As a trusted member of Richard II's inner circle, Edmund was left in charge of the kingdom when his nephew the king went on a military expedition to Ireland in 1399. Another nephew, Henry Bolingbroke, Duke of Lancaster, taking advantage of the king's absence, returned from exile in France and staged an invasion and *coup d'état*. Edmund acquiesced, effectively conniving in the overthrow of Richard II. Bolingbroke came to the throne as the first Lancastrian king, Henry IV (r.1399–1413).

Edmund was married to Isabella, one of the daughters of King Pedro I of Castile: she is said to have been temperamental and passionate, whereas he was mild-mannered and peaceable. Isabella became the subject of scandal over her affair with Richard II's half-brother John Holland, Earl of Huntingdon (d.1400). Her elder son, Edward (1373–1415), succeeded his father as Duke of York. Her second son was born at Conisbrough Castle and was consequently known

Left: This 1430s scene of a noblewoman's bedchamber shows many items similar to those mentioned in Maud's will: a bed with embroidered curtains, decorative wall-hangings, comfortable cushions, a gold belt and items of plate
Below: Maud's will mentions several items of personal decoration, including a gold cross, which might have resembled this 15th-century jewel found in Nottinghamshire – a gold pendant with a ruby in the centre

Countess Maud at Conisbrough

Maud Clifford's will describes the range of sumptuous possessions that once filled the finest rooms of Conisbrough Castle and adorned its rich inhabitants.

Richard of Conisbrough's second wife was Maud Clifford, daughter of the 8th Lord Clifford. They married in about 1413, but had no children and, after her husband's execution in 1415, Maud lived on at Conisbrough as her main residence until her own death in 1446. Countess Maud entertained her own family, the Cliffords, at Conisbrough, went to visit them at Skipton, and supported nearby Roche Abbey generously. Her will makes specific bequests of her most valuable goods, including fine textiles, handmade books, jewellery and plate, which must have been in her possession at Conisbrough. Among them are:

To Thomas, Lord Clifford, my relation:
- ✦ a 'hall' of Arras [fine woven wall-hanging from Arras, in modern Belgium], *bought from Sir Robert Babthorp*
- ✦ my red bed of Arras with three curtains
- ✦ four cushions of red silk
- ✦ two long cushions of cloth

To John Clifford, my godson:
- ✦ 12 silver dishes
- ✦ 6 salt-cellars signed with the 'trayfulles' [trefoils] and a shell

To Beatrice Waterton, my relation:
- ✦ a gold cross, which belonged to my mother
- ✦ my green Primary [a book of readings from the Bible]
- ✦ a diamond

To Katherine FitzWilliam:
- ✦ the brooch that I wear every day
- ✦ a small black Primary
- ✦ a jewel called Agnus Dei *covered with silver and written around with pearls*
- ✦ my best robe furred with miniver [white stoat fur]

To Maud Clifford, my god-daugter:
- ✦ my best gold belt

[no heading]
- ✦ my best furred robe with 'martes' [marten fur]

as Richard of Conisbrough (1385–1415); he was given the junior title of Earl of Cambridge. It might be that Richard of Conisbrough was actually John Holland's son, not Edmund's, which would explain why Edmund left him nothing in his will. Whatever the reason, Richard of Conisbrough became the only landless earl in England and lived at Conisbrough as his brother's tenant. He married Anne Mortimer, a descendant of Lionel, Duke of Clarence, Edward III's second son. Anne died in 1411, shortly after giving birth to their son, another Richard, who was probably also born at Conisbrough.

A Disastrous Plot

It may well have been resentment at his poverty that induced Richard of Conisbrough to hatch a plot to overthrow the new king, Henry V (r.1413–22). In 1415, Sir Thomas Grey and Lord Scrope of Masham met with Richard at Conisbrough Castle and together conspired to murder the king and to place Richard's brother-in-law Edmund Mortimer, Earl of March, on the throne. The plot was discovered and Richard found guilty of treason and executed. Richard's widow, his second wife, Maud Clifford, lived on at Conisbrough until her death in 1446.

When Richard of Conisbrough's elder brother, Edward, Duke of York, died at the Battle of Agincourt in 1415 without suffering injury (probably of a heart attack) the House of York's estates, including Conisbrough, were inherited by Richard's infant son, who succeeded his uncle as Duke of York. The richest landowner in England after the king, Richard of York (1411–60) was a direct descendant of two of Edward III's sons, and arguably had a better claim to the throne than the ruling House of Lancaster.

CONISBROUGH AND THE WARS OF THE ROSES

The government of Henry VI (r.1422–61; 1470–71) became increasingly unpopular in the 1450s for its corruption and incompetence, and its loss of the remaining English lands in France. When the king suffered a mental breakdown, royal authority collapsed. Civil war, known as the Wars of the Roses, broke out between the Lancastrian supporters of the king and the Yorkist rebels, led by Richard of York, who claimed the throne in 1460.

Richard was attainted (declared a traitor) and his estates seized in 1460, but his castles of Conisbrough and Sandal held out. Conisbrough was held by his supporter Edmund Talbot, who seized artillery from Sheffield Castle and mounted it on the walls. Richard unwisely emerged from Sandal Castle on 31 December 1460 and offered battle to a larger Lancastrian force; he was defeated and executed, and his head displayed on a spike over Micklegate Bar in York wearing a paper crown. Only three months later, at the Battle of Towton near Tadcaster, on 29 March 1461, Richard's 18-year-old son Edward, Earl of March, avenged his father, leading the Yorkist

Above: Contemporary painted glass portrait of Richard of York from the hall at Trinity College, Cambridge
Below: Edward, Earl of March, came to the throne as Edward IV in 1461; posthumous portrait of between about 1524 and 1556

'To cunesborow [Conisbrough] … by stony way and enclosid ground. Wher I saw no notable thing but the castel stonding on a rokket [rock] of stone and dichid [ditched]. The waulles of it hath be strong and full of toures [towers]'.
John Leland, *Itinerary*, 1539–43

forces in a terrible massacre of the Lancastrian army: it was the bloodiest battle ever fought on English soil.

Edward of March now ascended the throne as Edward IV (r.1461–70; 1471–83), and Conisbrough thus became Crown property. This, however lessened, rather than increased, the castle's importance: from being a principal residence of the House of York, Conisbrough was now just one royal castle among many, with relatively cramped and limited accommodation. The Yorkist triumph meant that Conisbrough would never again be occupied as a major residence, and within two generations it had fallen into ruin.

THE CASTLE ABANDONED

The last recorded repairs to Conisbrough Castle were carried out in 1482–3 under Richard III (r.1483–5), Richard of York's fourth and youngest son. Thereafter it seems to have been virtually abandoned.

In 1538 a survey of Conisbrough and Tickhill castles was carried out for Henry VIII (r.1509–47) by three commissioners, Thomas Fairfax, Thomas Green and Francis Frobisher. They were advised by three craftsmen: John Foreman (a mason), Thomas Jackson (a plumber) and John Thomson (a carpenter). They found that the gates and bridge had collapsed, together with the south curtain wall, as it appears today. Some of the great tower's floors were intact but one had collapsed, its roof was decayed, and its well was full of gravel. There was no

Above: An 1824 engraving of John Leland (c.1503–52) by Thomas Charles Wageman, after a contemporary portrait by Hans Holbein

Right: By the time Samuel Buck made this engraving of Conisbrough in 1725, the castle was already largely ruined and appeared much as it does today. One exception was the long, straight flight of steps shown leading to the entrance of the great tower. This is evidently not an original feature, but it is not clear when it was built

artillery in the castle and, ominously for its future, the stone of its walls was valued at £200. It is clear that the castle was falling into ruin, and had no contents of any value. The accompanying survey of Tickhill mentions its lodgings and service buildings, but none of the buildings in Conisbrough's inner bailey is mentioned, suggesting that those which had survived the collapse of the south curtain wall had already been demolished. Most of their walls were taken down to ground level, suggesting that the inner bailey buildings had been systematically dismantled for their materials.

In 1559 Elizabeth I (r.1558–1603) granted the castle and manor of Conisbrough to her cousin Henry Carey, Lord Hunsdon (1526–1596). The estate remained with his family until Lady Mary Carey, his great-great-granddaughter, married William Heveningham in 1655. The castle was not touched in the Civil War and Commonwealth period, doubtless because it was already an indefensible ruin.

William and Lady Mary's granddaughter Carey Newton married Edward Coke (1676–1707) of Holkham in Norfolk, and it was he who owned it when the artist Samuel Buck visited Conisbrough in 1725. Buck's engraving, the earliest known view of the castle, shows it in almost exactly the same state as it appears today, with the great tower and bailey walls standing, but with a large gap in the curtain wall to the west, the gatehouse and the whole south curtain wall gone, and only a few walls of the bailey buildings remaining.

Above: Portrait of Henry Carey, 1st Baron Hunsdon, who was granted Conisbrough in 1559; by Marcus Gheeraerts the Younger (c.1561–1636)

Top: Portrait miniature by Edward
Tayler of Marcia Pelham (1863–1926),
4th Countess of Yarborough, who
inherited Conisbrough in 1888
Above: Photograph of Sackville George
Pelham (1888–1948), 5th Earl of
Yarborough, son and heir of Marcia
Pelham, taken in 1938
Below: A May Day celebration at
Conisbrough, early 20th century

A PICTURESQUE RUIN

In 1737 the manor of Conisbrough was sold to Thomas
Osborne, 4th Duke of Leeds, a major Yorkshire landowner. By
the early 19th century the castle's fame was spreading, and
several engravings of it were published. Sir Walter Scott's novel
Ivanhoe (1819) first made it famous, while the Revd Joseph
Hunter's *History of Doncaster* (1828) provided the first
scholarly account of Conisbrough's history. In 1849 the railway
came to Conisbrough with the opening of a line from
Doncaster to Swinton, and the castle became a popular tourist
destination. A 'Missionary Gathering' of over 5,000 people was
held here in 1853, and the children of the Doncaster Union
Workhouse visited the castle in July 1858. The castle was also
attracting the attention of antiquaries, with a visit by the British
Archaeological Association in 1873, and the publication of
GT Clark's research on the castle in 1883.

On the death of the 6th Duke of Leeds in 1838, Conisbrough
was left to his only daughter, Charlotte, and his son-in-law,
Sackville Lane-Fox (d.1874). On the death of the 7th Duke in
1859, Lane-Fox also inherited the ancient baronies of Conyers
and Darcy, becoming the 11th Lord Conyers. These estates
and titles passed to his son Sackville George Lane-Fox, 12th
Lord Conyers (d.1888). His daughter and heiress Marcia
inherited the manor and castle of Conisbrough, which passed
on her death in 1926 to her son, the 5th Earl of Yarborough.

The castle's setting changed greatly in the late 19th century,
the town of Conisbrough growing dramatically thanks to the
opening of coal mines at Denaby Main (1863–8) and Cadeby
(1893). The castle and its park became an important amenity
for the growing town, and its owners took better care of it.
The 12th Lord Conyers repaired the ruins, and it was either he
or his daughter Marcia who built the wall around the castle
park, together with the present entrance lodge and gates, in
the late 19th century.

Sir Walter Scott and *Ivanhoe*

Sir Walter Scott (1771–1832) was the most prolific and successful novelist of his age, and his works reached a mass audience.

Scott's 'Waverley Novels' set new standards of accuracy and scholarship in their evocation of the past: he took a great interest in medieval monuments, and used a number of them as settings for his novels. In December 1811 he wrote to his friend, the antiquary JSB Morritt: 'Do you know anything of a striking, ancient castle belonging I think to the Duke of Leeds called Coningburgh Castle? I once flew past it in the mail coach, when its round tower and flying buttresses had a most romantic effect in the morning dawn.'

Scott was inspired by Conisbrough to set his most popular novel *Ivanhoe* (1819) in South Yorkshire and Leicestershire, in which the

castle figures as the seat of the Saxon lord Athelstane: '*There are few more beautiful or striking scenes in England that are presented by the vicinity of this ancient Saxon fortress … On a mount ascending from the river, well defended by walls and ditches, rises this ancient edifice, which, as the name implies, was, previous to the Conquest, a royal*

residence of the kings of England' (*Ivanhoe*, Chapter 41).

Sir Walter was correct about the derivation of the name 'Conisbrough' (though he calls it 'Coningsburgh' in his book), but incorrect about the castle's Saxon date. In 1830 his son Major Walter Scott was staying in the area: the author asked his son to make a drawing of the castle to help the illustrator who was producing engravings for a new edition of the book.

Top: Richard I and Ivanhoe arriving at 'Coningsburgh' – engraving by JC Bentley, 1837, of a drawing by H Melville. Conisbrough's great tower and St Peter's church appear above the trees
Above: *Sir Walter Scott by Edwin Landseer, 1824*

Above: The Ministry of Works undertaking clearing and consolidation work in the inner bailey at Conisbrough, May 1951

Below: This green glazed vase in the shape of the great tower was made in nearby Mexborough in the mid 19th century. Conisbrough Castle's great tower remains an iconic local landmark

CONISBROUGH IN THE 20TH CENTURY

The castle remained a popular visitor attraction in the early 20th century, and an important symbol and amenity for the town. On 8 July 1912, George V (r.1910–36) and Queen Mary visited Conisbrough, taking tea in a marquee attended by 3,600 children of the Conisbrough and Denaby schools and the Denaby Main troop of scouts. In 1946 the 5th Earl of Yarborough sold the castle to Conisbrough Urban District Council for £25. Maintaining it was a considerable burden, and in 1950 it was taken into guardianship by the Ministry of Works. The Ministry carried out major repairs, and in 1967–9 undertook major archaeological investigations in order to improve knowledge and understanding of the building. The work was directed by Michael Thompson, who uncovered the remains of the bailey buildings and reconstructed their plan. Stephen Johnson directed four more seasons of archaeology in 1973–7, rediscovering and clearing the collapsed remains of the gatehouse and the south curtain wall.

In 1984 Conisbrough passed into the care of English Heritage, which, in the 1990s, worked with Doncaster Metropolitan Borough Council and a local charitable trust to manage the site. The great tower was re-roofed and floored in 1993–5 to protect it from the weather and improve public access, while a new exhibition centre was built. In 2007 the castle reverted to management by English Heritage, and since then further enhancements, including the opening of a new exhibition and shop in the Victorian lodge building, have followed, with support from the Borough Council and the Heritage Lottery Fund.